EDGE
BOOKS

Epic Disasters

THE WORST
WILDFIRES
OF ALL TIME

by Suzanne Garbe

Consultant:
Susan L. Cutter, PhD
Director
Hazards and Vulnerability Research Institute
University of South Carolina

CAPSTONE PRESS
a capstone imprint

Edge Books are published by Capstone Press,
1710 Roe Crest Drive, North Mankato, Minnesota 56003.
www.capstonepub.com

Library of Congress Cataloging-in-Publication Data
Garbe, Suzanne.
    The worst wildfires of all time / by Suzanne Garbe.
    p. cm.—(Edge books. Epic disasters)
    Includes bibliographical references and index.
    Summary: "Describes the worst wildfires in history, as well as causes, types,
and disaster tips"—Provided by publisher.
    ISBN 978-1-4296-8418-7 (library binding)
    ISBN 978-1-62065-222-0 (ebook PDF)
1. Wildfires—Juvenile literature. I. Title.
SD421.23.G37 2013
363.34'9—dc23   2011053150

Editorial Credits
Anthony Wacholtz, editor; Gene Bentdahl, designer; Marcie Spence,
    media researcher; Laura Manthe, production specialist

Photo Credits
Alamy Images: David R. Frazier Photolibrary, Inc., 16, Michael Anhaeuser, 11,
Paul Mayall, 25, Reuters, 18; AP Images: Alaska Fire Service, 21; Corbis: 7,
Andrew Gombert, 28, Jonathan Blair, 14, Michael S. Yamashita, 9, NASA/CNP,
27; Shutterstock: Jim Parkin, 23, Peter Weber, 17, Phillip Holland, 29, Roger
Rosentreter, cover, 1, 5; Wikimedia, 13

Printed in the United States of America in Stevens Point, Wisconsin.
032012   006678WZF12

TABLE of CONTENTS

A FIERY THREAT

A wall of fire rushes through a forest faster than a speeding car. It leaps from treetop to treetop. Ash rains down from the sky. The roar of the fire makes it impossible to hear. With the fire come winds that feel as strong as a hurricane's.

These are just a few ways witnesses have described wildfires. A wildfire is any uncontrolled fire that happens in nature. Wildfires are a threat all over the world. They can run through fields and blaze across forests. They can burn for hours or for months. They can spread into villages and cities.

Sometimes the causes of wildfires can be hard to determine. They can be started by natural causes, including lightning and volcanic activity. Most wildfires, however, are caused by humans. Sometimes people set fires on purpose. Other times, the fires are accidental.

Wildfires are necessary for most ecosystems. They keep a forest's plant and animal life in balance. If fires are prevented, dry **vegetation** can build up. The resulting **litter** can make the threat of fire worse. Some plants even need wildfires to reproduce. The pinecones of the Lodgepole Pine only release their seeds after being burned.

vegetation—plant life
litter—dead and decaying material on the ground in forested areas

Although most wildfires are minor and burn themselves out, a small percentage threaten people. The worst wildfires are remembered years after the final flame goes out.

TYPES OF WILDFIRES

There are three main types of wildfires:

- Surface fires are fast fires that burn leaves and small branches near the ground. They usually aren't a risk to older trees because they move so quickly through the area.

- Ground fires are slow-moving fires. They creep through the litter layer and soil, especially during long periods of drought. They can kill both large and small trees because of the high heat. Ground fires can burn for weeks or months.

- Crown fires burn in the tops of trees, causing branches and embers to fall and spread the fire along the ground. Crown fires are often caused by ground or surface fires. Crown fires are so hot that they can create their own wind, which feeds the fire.

PESHTIGO FIRE

DATE: October 8, 1871
LOCATION: Wisconsin and Michigan
AREA BURNED: 3,780,000 acres
(1.5 million hectares)

In the fall of 1871, the midwestern United States was in the middle of a 14-week **drought**. The drought created perfect conditions for fire across the Upper Midwest. One place ripe for fire was Peshtigo, Wisconsin. It was a successful but quiet lumber town with about 1,700 people. On October 8, 1871, a brush fire **ignited**.

The fire came upon the town of Peshtigo suddenly. Some people claimed less than 10 minutes passed between the first building burning and the whole village catching fire. One witness wrote, "The roar increased and burning coals began to drop ... first like stray meteors of the night, and then as thickly as the snows of winter ... The wind reached the force of a tornado, the buildings nearest the woods were on fire, and the very air seemed an atmosphere of flames."

In less than an hour, Peshtigo was almost completely destroyed. Only one building was still standing the next day. At least 1,500 people lost their lives. The fire was one of the deadliest wildfires in history.

drought—a long period of weather with little or no rainfall
ignite—to set fire to something

THE GREAT CHICAGO FIRE

The Great Chicago Fire is one of the most well-known fires in U.S. history. It also started on October 8, 1871. The Chicago fire drew attention away from the Peshtigo Fire, even though the Peshtigo Fire took many more lives. The Great Chicago Fire killed at least 300 people and left 500,000 more homeless.

FACT:
Fires need three things in order to burn: heat, fuel, and oxygen. Many wildfires happen in forests because trees, fallen branches, and dead leaves provide wildfires with a lot of fuel.

FIRE IN INDONESIA

DATE: 1997-1998
LOCATION: Indonesia
AREA BURNED: about 20 million acres (8.1 million hectares)

Fire is often used as a method to clear land for farming. In Indonesia, this practice turned into a disaster. In 1997 large companies and farmers were burning farmland and lost control of the fires. Drought conditions spread the flames across the islands of Sumatra, Borneo, Sulawesi, and Java. Smoke and other **pollutants** filled the sky. Wind spread the smog to other countries, including Malaysia, Thailand, and Singapore. The fires were so large and covered so much area that they could be seen from space.

The Indonesian government was slow to respond to the crisis. The fires continued to burn into 1998. The intense smog caused **respiratory** diseases and other health problems for people across the region.

pollutant—a harmful material that can damage the environment
respiratory—related to breathing

Small farmers lost their crops to the spreading fire. One farmer who was trying to fight the blaze said that "as soon as it stops in one place it starts in another." In the end, about 20 million acres (8.1 million hectares) of land was burned. It was one of the largest wildfires in recorded history.

HISTORY THREATENED

DATE: June-September 2007
LOCATION: Greece
AREA BURNED: about 670,000 acres
(271,000 hectares)

Although wildfires can be natural and necessary to ecosystems, they don't always have natural causes. In the summer of 2007, multiple fires broke out in Greece. Some of them were started by **arsonists.** The blazes grew into the worst wildfires in Greece's recorded history. The dry summer and intense heat helped the fires spread. People in the worst-hit region became trapped in their homes while fire licked at their front steps. Greece, with help from the European Union, launched a huge rescue effort. Emergency teams arrived in helicopters to rescue people from their houses. Special airplanes dropped water on the fires.

arsonist—a person who intentionally and illegally sets property on fire

These efforts saved many people. But the wildfires burned about 670,000 acres (271,000 hectares)—a section of forest bigger than Rhode Island. Eighty-four people were killed. At least 110 villages were burned to the ground. The ancient city of Olympia, home of the first Olympic Games, barely escaped destruction.

FACT:
Airplanes were first used to fight fires in the 1930s. Pilots dropped wooden barrels full of water from planes.

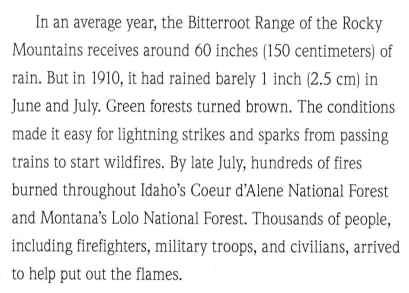

DATE: August 1910

LOCATION: Idaho, Montana, and western Canada

AREA BURNED: 3 million acres (1.2 million hectares)

In an average year, the Bitterroot Range of the Rocky Mountains receives around 60 inches (150 centimeters) of rain. But in 1910, it had rained barely 1 inch (2.5 cm) in June and July. Green forests turned brown. The conditions made it easy for lightning strikes and sparks from passing trains to start wildfires. By late July, hundreds of fires burned throughout Idaho's Coeur d'Alene National Forest and Montana's Lolo National Forest. Thousands of people, including firefighters, military troops, and civilians, arrived to help put out the flames.

By mid-August, officials started to think the fires were under control. But on August 20, a cold front came through. Winds rushed in at 75 miles (121 kilometers) per hour. The winds fed more oxygen to the flames. The fires expanded and merged into giant blazes.

The huge fires were overwhelming. Firefighters struggled to contain them. In the end, heavy rains and low temperatures helped put out the fires on August 23. About 85 people lost their lives. Three million acres (1.2 million hectares) had been destroyed in the Big Burn, making it one of the largest wildfires in U.S. history.

FACT:
Tens of thousands of wildfires happen each year in the United States. Most of them are small. In 2010, 71,971 wildfires burned 3,422,723 acres (1,385,127 hectares) of U.S. soil. That's an average of about 48 acres (19 hectares) per fire.

THE SUMMER OF FIRE

DATE: June–September 1988

LOCATION: Yellowstone National Park in Wyoming, Montana, and Idaho

AREA BURNED: 1.2 million acres (486,000 hectares)

On June 14, 1988, a small fire sparked just outside Yellowstone National Park. No one expected the blaze would be the first of many to rage throughout Yellowstone that summer. Over the next three months, the fires became one of the most famous outbreaks in American history.

Yellowstone National Park became the world's first national park in 1872. The land where the park sits has always been shaped by fire. By 1988 scientists knew that wildfires were an important part of many forest ecosystems. So when lightning sparked fires around Yellowstone that summer, park rangers let them go. However, it was the driest summer the park had ever recorded.

By July 21 officials realized the fires were getting too large and might threaten buildings and people. Firefighters began attacking the fires, but they couldn't keep up. In the last two weeks of July, the amount of land burned jumped from 8,500 acres (3,400 hectares) to 99,000 acres (40,000 hectares). One month later, the fires were still burning. On August 20 strong winds pushed the flames over 150,000 acres (61,000 hectares). The day became known as "Black Saturday."

By late August parts of the park were closed to visitors. People in nearby towns feared the fires would spread. More than 25,000 firefighters worked to put out the fires. It wasn't until rain and snow arrived in September that the fires started to die down. The last flames were finally put out in November. The Yellowstone fire of 1988 continues to be one of the most well-known fires in U.S. history.

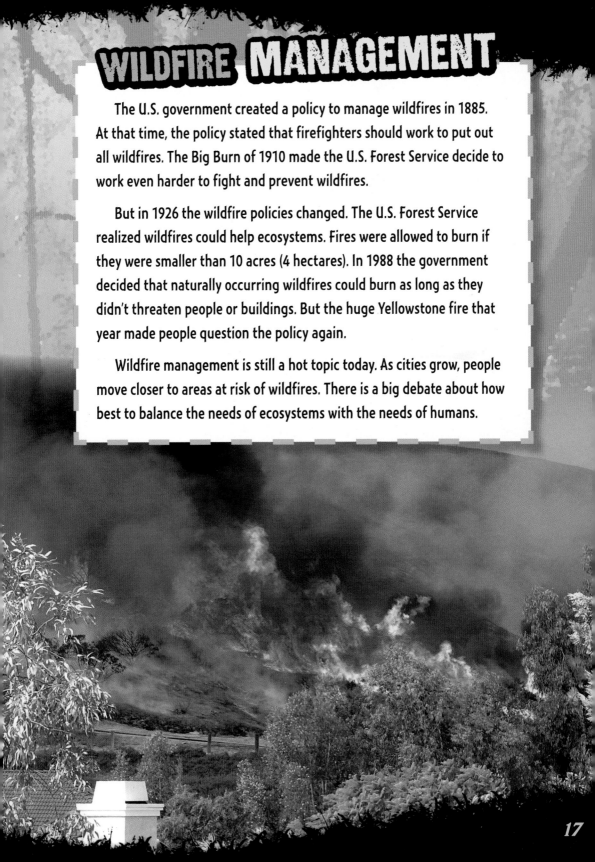

WILDFIRE MANAGEMENT

The U.S. government created a policy to manage wildfires in 1885. At that time, the policy stated that firefighters should work to put out all wildfires. The Big Burn of 1910 made the U.S. Forest Service decide to work even harder to fight and prevent wildfires.

But in 1926 the wildfire policies changed. The U.S. Forest Service realized wildfires could help ecosystems. Fires were allowed to burn if they were smaller than 10 acres (4 hectares). In 1988 the government decided that naturally occurring wildfires could burn as long as they didn't threaten people or buildings. But the huge Yellowstone fire that year made people question the policy again.

Wildfire management is still a hot topic today. As cities grow, people move closer to areas at risk of wildfires. There is a big debate about how best to balance the needs of ecosystems with the needs of humans.

FIRE IN SIBERIA

DATE: spring and summer 2003
LOCATION: Siberia, Russia
AREA BURNED: 46.7 million acres
(18.9 million hectares)

Forest land in Siberia, Russia, makes up about one-fifth of the world's forests. In recent years, the temperatures in those Siberian forests have changed dramatically. Temperatures are rising twice as fast as average temperatures around the world. At the same time, Siberia has seen more wildfires than ever before. In the past, one particular spot would experience wildfires once every 100 years. Now they happen every 65 years. Some scientists think climate change is responsible.

The spring and summer of 2003 saw Russia's largest wildfires in more than 100 years. The region had been unusually dry that spring. Additionally, Russian officials believe many fires were set by timber thieves to cover their tracks. Whatever the reason, thousands of fires raged across the region that spring and summer. By the end, more than 46.7 million acres (18.9 million hectares) had burned. For weeks, a smoky haze covered much of Russia, Mongolia, and China. Smoke from the fires traveled to Japan and even the United States.

AMERICA'S BIGGEST WILDFIRE

DATE: summer 2004
LOCATION: Alaska
AREA BURNED: 6.75 million acres
(2.73 million hectares)

The summer of 2004 was unusually hot and dry in Alaska. Hundreds of wildfires were sparked and began to grow out of control. One group of wildfires, known as the Taylor Complex, burned 1.3 million acres (526,000 hectares) alone.

Most of the fires that summer were in remote areas. However, some houses about 30 miles (48 km) from the city of Fairbanks were threatened. Firefighters and state troopers made phone calls and went door-to-door to warn residents to head to Fairbanks for safety. But even the city wasn't untouched by the fire. So much smoke poured into Fairbanks that officials advised residents to wear masks if they went outside.

When the fires finally ended later that summer, 6.75 million acres (2.73 million hectares) had burned. It was the largest wildfire in U.S. history. Luckily, no one was killed.

FACT:
Firefighters sometimes talk about single fires and complex fires. If single fires are close together, they're called a complex fire. This means that firefighters will manage and fight them together like one fire.

MIRAMICHI FIRE

DATE: 1825

LOCATION: Maine and Miramichi, New Brunswick, Canada

AREA BURNED: 3 million acres (1.2 million hectares)

Unsafe **logging** practices have been known to cause many wildfires. Perhaps the worst example is the Miramichi fire of 1825. At that time, loggers often took only the best wood and left the scraps behind. This created a serious fire hazard because the scraps could easily catch fire.

No one knows what triggered the wildfire on October 7, 1825. It could have been the small fires farmers set to clear their fields. In any case, human actions helped the fire grow and spread. Within just a few days, 3 million acres (1.2 million hectares) of forest were burned and at least 160 people were killed.

logging—cutting down trees to make lumber and paper

PRESCRIBED BURNS

Today many fire officials start fires in wild areas on purpose. They do this to burn vegetation and other natural fuel so uncontrolled wildfires won't start later. This type of wildfire is called a prescribed burn.

Firefighters closely watch a prescribed burn in Utah.

BLACK SATURDAY BUSHFIRES

DATE: February 7, 2009
LOCATION: Victoria, Australia
AREA BURNED: 1.1 million acres (445,000 hectares)

In February 2009, Australia was in the midst of a very hot, dry summer. The state of Victoria was experiencing the worst drought in a century. By early February, temperatures had been above 100 degrees Fahrenheit (38 degrees Celsius) for several days. Small fires had already been burning for weeks.

On February 7, things got worse. Strong winds caused a **firestorm** to sweep across the land. The flames came too quickly for anyone to prepare. The fires raged across more than 1 million acres (405,000 hectares) of land. Ash rained down from the sky. Thousands of firefighters worked to get the fires under control, but it took several days.

When the fires finally stopped burning, many farms had been turned to ashes. Blackened tree trunks were all that remained of forests. The iron roofs of houses were twisted from the heat. Several towns were destroyed, and the remains of burned-out cars lined roads. At least 750 homes burned down, and 173 people were dead. The Black Saturday Bushfires became the deadliest fires in Australian history.

FACT:

Victoria was also home to another famous wildfire, the Black Friday Bushfires, in 1939. These fires had less than half the death toll of the 2009 fires but were much larger. They burned about 5 million acres (2 million hectares) of land.

firestorm—a violent and intense fire

CEDAR FIRE

DATE: October 25-28, 2003
LOCATION: near San Diego, California
AREA BURNED: 280,000 acres (113,000 hectares)

On October 25, 2003, Sergio Martinez was hunting in the woods near San Diego, California. He became separated from his hunting partner and wandered through the trees. As hours passed, he ran out of water and began to panic. "I didn't want my body to be found in a ravine," he later said. "The thirst was sucking the life out of me." He needed a way to signal his location to rescuers. So he lit a small fire and waited for help.

The fire quickly grew out of control. At 5:30 that night, it covered 20 acres (8.1 hectares). Less than seven hours later, it had grown to 5,500 acres (2,230 hectares). By 3:00 a.m. on October 26, it had raged across 62,000 acres (25,100 hectares). By 6:30 a.m., the blaze had traveled into the city of San Diego.

The Cedar Fire burned more than 280,000 acres (113,000 hectares) of land in San Diego County. It destroyed 2,820 buildings and caused 15 deaths. It is the largest single wildfire in California history.

an aerial view of the Cedar Fire

TIMELINE

OCTOBER 25, 2003, 5:37 P.M.: The Cedar Fire is reported.

11:18 P.M.: Flames between 75 and 100 feet (23 and 30 meters) high are reported.

OCTOBER 26, 2003, 8:27 A.M.: The wind changes direction, causing the path of the fire to change.

10:00 A.M.: All off-duty firefighters in San Diego are requested to assist with the fire.

OCTOBER 27, 2003, 10:00 P.M.: The fire is estimated to cover 193,646 acres (78,366 hectares).

OCTOBER 28, 2003: The fire is contained.

LIVING WITH WILDFIRES

If your house is in an area at risk for wildfires, you can take steps to stay safe. You probably know it's important to have working smoke and carbon monoxide alarms throughout your home. But there are other steps you can take too:

- Keep a fire extinguisher handy, and know how to use it.
- If your house is near a pine forest, keep 100 feet (30 m) clear between your home and the forest.
- Rake regularly so leaves, twigs, and other **flammable** vegetation isn't near the house.
- Buy a garden hose long enough to reach all parts of the house.
- Create a disaster plan with your family that includes where to go and what to do in case of a wildfire.
- Create a survival kit in case you get trapped.

A firefighter covers a house with a foam that will prevent the building from catching fire.

If a wildfire warning is issued for your area, take these additional steps. Find an **evacuation** route that leads away from the fire. Move furniture that might catch fire to the center of the home. Put on protective clothing, including long pants, long-sleeved shirts, sturdy shoes, and gloves. Evacuate immediately if you are told to do so.

The biggest danger in a fire is the smoke, not the flames. If your house fills with smoke, get on the floor and crawl to safety.

As dangerous as wildfires can be, they also play an important part in nature. Wildfires cause destruction, but they also usher in new life. Studying wildfires helps us see how important—and dangerous— wildfires can be.

flammable—able to burn
evacuation—the removal of large numbers of people from an area during a time of danger

GLOSSARY

arsonist (AR-suhn-ist)—a person who intentionally and illegally sets property on fire

drought (DROUT)—a long period of weather with little or no rainfall

ecosystem (EE-koh-sis-tuhm)—a system of living and nonliving things in an environment

evacuation (i-va-kyuh-WAY-shun)—the removal of large numbers of people from an area during a time of danger

firestorm (FIRE-storm)—a violent and intense fire

flammable (FLA-muh-buhl)—able to burn

hazard (HAZ-urd)—something that is dangerous

ignite (ig-NITE)—to set fire to something

litter (LIT-ur)—dead and decaying material on the ground in forested areas

logging (LAW-ging)—the cutting down of trees to make lumber and paper

pollutant (puh-LOOT-uhnt)—a harmful material that can damage the environment

respiratory (RESS-pi-ruh-taw-ree)—related to the process of breathing

vegetation (vej-uh-TAY-shuhn)—plant life

READ MORE

Levy, Janey. *World's Worst Fires.* Deadly Disasters. New York: PowerKids Press, 2009.

Silverstein, Alvin, Virginia Silverstein, and Laura Silverstein Nunn. *Wildfires: The Science Behind Raging Infernos.* Science behind Natural Disasters. Berkeley Heights, N.J.: Enslow Publishers, 2010.

Sirota, Lyn A. *Out of Control: The Science of Wildfires.* Headline Science. Minneapolis: Compass Point Books, 2009.

Trammel, Howard K. *Wildfires.* Earth Science. New York: Children's Press, 2009.

INTERNET SITES

FactHound offers a safe, fun way to find Internet sites related to this book. All of the sites on FactHound have been researched by our staff.

Here's all you do:

Visit *www.facthound.com*

Type in this code: 9781429684187

Check out projects, games and lots more at
www.capstonekids.com

INDEX